lines to connect the dots
●●●●●●●●●●●●●●●●●●●●●●

CHRISTOPHER FEATHERSTON

Copyright © 2021 by Christopher Featherston
All rights reserved. This book or any portion thereof may not be reproduced or used in any manner whatsoever without the express written permission of the publisher except for the use of brief quotations in a book review.

Illustrations by Rosemarie Spracklin

*Dedicated to Kennedy Reese Featherston.
Always be yourself and never settle.*

Table of Contents
Masculinity............2
Dependency.........14
Boundaries...........24
Heartbreak...........52
Motivation............61
Love......................86
Peace...................109
Success..............139
Life......................151

The Most High presides over everything, even Satan which is just another word for adversary, but our adversary, not God's. The Devil indirectly serves God by acting as a filter of deceptions to show God who really follows his word. The presence of evil balances out the scale, which is vital. Too much bad is horrible, but too much good is bad as well. God operates on a scale that we can't fully comprehend. A scale where our big picture is just a small part of his. Where Satan himself is just a pawn in his plan. There's a technique ballet dancers use called spotting, it's when they focus on a constant point while executing various turns to prevent dizziness. As this world turns, we need spotting more than ever with the constant point being God. The Devil is only after you because he's threatened by you. He keeps his grasp on you through convenience. Most of the time, the easy way is a dead end. Whenever God gives you something real, the Devil will tempt you with delusions of perfection. Make sure that you know better. You can't move in sync with your spirit when you're overly attached to materials of the flesh.

To play God is to mimic the Devil.

When you stop seeking glory and start giving it to God, his glory will begin to channel through you as a worthy bridge. People tend to avoid God because with God comes structure, with structure comes boundaries and rules, and with rules come accountability. We kill our idols to escape that accountability and any real growth into our full potential, because we are comfortable in sin. A giant will always appear to walk slowly through the eyes of an ant. But in that same breath, the ant can't outrun one of those slow steps in a 1,000 strides. In other words, be careful judging a person who's taking their time. In most cases, that slow step is calculated, will equate to success, and speak directly to longevity. The bigger the picture, the more space you need to create to see it in its entirety. Our sense of free will presides within God's foresight and conveys our fate effortlessly. Sometimes problems only seem big because you're in the middle of it. Separate yourself, make it small enough to dissect, and solve it properly.

Have you ever been walking across the street with one of your parents and they snatched you back to save you from getting hit by a car? That's how God works in our lives sometimes. It may seem like you're being held back or going backwards, but it's really for your benefit in the long run. From time to time, God will bring tears to your eyes to water the seed you planted, and use your enemies to throw dirt on it. A tree needs a little wind to pull the seed from its limbs, then that seed also needs water to grow. Remember that the next time you're in a storm...

When it comes to the issues between men and women, a great deal of onus must be focused on the fact that most men don't know their worth. When a man doesn't know the power he possesses, he will abuse it and those around him in ignorance. Men are raised to measure their worth from what they can conquer but are never taught how to rule from within.

How a king rules over himself is just as important as how he leads his people.

A lot of men don't know their role in the world, which leads to a subconscious improvisation of what they think exudes manhood. This lack of foundation causes a diminished self respect, and when that respect isn't there, forethought isn't either. So men will run a muck because as he thinks little of his actions he will also think little of the effects that follow.

Boys fantasize, men realize.

The crown isn't always placed upon your head, sometimes it's pulled up from over your eyes...

You can't be a king and a victim at the same time. A king will never be a victim, even in defeat, because a true king keeps accountability even in loss. Lack of accountability is a lazy man's sport. It deflects blame to a shallow level of your hurt, the quickest most convenient route. Rather than diving deeper past the surface level issues towards the source being yourself.

*If you aren't leading by example,
you aren't leading at all.*

*It's one thing to spoil a woman.
It's another to preserve her...*

Men, providing isn't just materialistic. Can you provide physical, mental, and spiritual protection, insight, guidance, companionship, and love?

Every pretty woman that you come across isn't meant to be approached. Just like every flower isn't to be picked, it'll die if you don't have your pot and soil ready. Same goes for women, admire her and know when to keep it at that.

The woman is God's gift to man, not momma's boy, liar, etc. You have to be a man first to truly receive a woman's true potential.

A woman doesn't belong with a man who belongs to the world. Because a man who belongs to the world, doesn't know where he belongs. So he is easily influenced by it. A man shouldn't belong to the world because the world belongs to him. And with the right woman, it wouldn't be long before the world is his.

Men, just because women are emotionally driven, doesn't mean that you need to match her. What makes her beautiful won't do the same for you. Come to understand women and stay within your logic so you can complement rather than counteract.

It's not necessarily sensitivity that women want. it's more so honesty of inevitable feelings and emotion. That openness exudes confidence, sparks intrigue, and makes them feel more secure as they know exactly what they're dealing with...

A woman's naturally negative polarity pushes a man to his full potential. A man's naturally positive polarity keeps her grounded by balancing her out.

She presents the problem to a man that's supposed to be able to solve it. He shows her how capable and beautiful that she already is.

Survivors are naturally essential, but they don't make for good leaders. If it came down to it, they'd conform and assimilate to their surroundings rather than fight and possibly die to dictate them. Women are survivors, they naturally adapt to preserve themselves. This is a vital characteristic, but alone, doesn't foster good leadership. Men and women are made to lead their people together. Men should protect women so they don't have to try to fit into a society that doesn't value them. It's not up to the woman to change, they're doing what they have to do with what they're given. Just because a woman is attracted to your success doesn't always mean she wants your money. Your success shows her that you can plan, execute, and lead. Every woman is submissive by nature, but she can't be when she's too busy providing. The woman is the most aligned with her purpose as a wife and a mother. This nature is no longer a safe place for them because it's been taken for granted, and advantage of, by men who've drifted from their nature to provide and protect.

*The man is supposed to **protect the woman**, even if it's from himself...*

When you depend on someone else for happiness, the potential for heartbreak is magnified. When you lose them, you lose the medication to the lacking that you could've remedied through solitude and self reflection. But now you're misplacing the bad state within the current disconnection that you're experiencing, which pushes your flaws deeper into excuses, further from accountability, and right into the hands of your demons.

When we run from our demons, as we look back, we risk bumping into the wrong people...

Understand that your demons love it when you jump romantically from person to person instead of dealing with them. They'll even block and hide red flags to keep you blind, knowing the potential for issues and heartbreak will only give them more company and increase their influence.

Take a break to break their hold.

*We get what we deserve in life. When you take responsibility or in other words, response ability. You think back and realize that you ultimately made your own choices in every situation, but you just responded wrong. After you embrace those past mistakes they won't demand so much of your attention, you'll gain clarity, and make yourself easier to love. Killing **your demo**ns, giving less to run from and more to run to...*

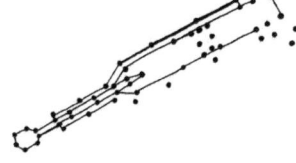

*Filling voids with things is hoarding.
Filling voids with people is imprisonment.*

You can't expect to find your soulmate when you haven't done any soul searching...

Thirst and dishonesty will move in lock step as a lonely desperate person is quicker to lie out of fear of losing someone. Not worried about acceptance, a truly confident person will be more honest. They only want what's for them and they won't get that by lying, or not being themselves. Stop looking for your worth through other people's eyes. When you seek acceptance before knowledge of self, it pushes you into a cycle instead of knowing yourself. **And embracing people that fit with *you*.**

The problem is that you're looking for someone to act right, and that's exactly what you're getting, people who know how to act...

People who take anything just to say that they're taken, find themselves taken for granted and taken advantage of, then they end up taking what they've taken into their next relationship...

Stop dancing with people who don't move in harmony with your vibration.

Stop confusing lust with chemistry. It's only one ingredient, not the entire pot. And just because you have chemistry doesn't mean it's productive. Sometimes your demons are just compatible. Following the pack isn't always just about fitting in, it's about hiding out as well. A lot of people are running from something. Be careful out here, many people are lonely and seeking solace in your company. They're actually far from alone, crowded with demons, and trying to find someone to share the load with. Solitude is an intelligent man's sport and forever frightening to everyone else. A buffoon is always bored because it isn't about the empty room, it's about the empty head space.

Asking for a handout isn't just about money and opportunity. People do it with love and peace as well, the success rate is just the same. You have to give it to yourself first and foremost. You have to love yourself before you can attract real love. You're doing without because you're starting outside of yourself. The energy that you use reaching for another person's hand can be put into pulling yourself up. Of course we all could use a helping hand sometimes. Don't rely on it, let it be a surprising bonus to the work that you're already putting in.

*Be careful trying to fill a **void, you might fall in**. Grow into it instead.*

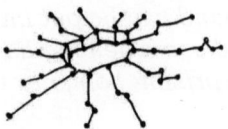

Anything that's hurt will act out of desperation, clinging on to everything that gets close out of fear of becoming more hurt or being left for dead. There's nothing wrong or right about that, but it leaves you with nothing, until you realize that nothing can help you but you. When you're looking for something, whatever you discover first gives you a sense of accomplishment, that can easily be confused for success. This won't always be the same depending on what you're looking for. The misguided sense of success when looking for something will sometimes cause you to settle for quick gratification rather than digging deeper for the actual treasures.

When you're seeking a relationship, or anything, if you're lacking vision, you're left with emotions basically feeling your way through. It's like walking into a dark room reaching to feel something, anything. When you finally reach a simple cup, the feeling of salvation is exaggerated, but you're not even close to a light switch. Then have the nerve to be disappointed when you realize that you're still sitting in the dark. When you have a vision, you can feel with purpose. So if you grab anything other than a light switch, you'll know it isn't for you from the beginning and continue on until you find something that actually sheds the light that you're looking for.

Your worth isn't something that you find, it's something you build. It's wrapped around what you tolerate, and without boundaries, you're in no shape to be valued.

Your big picture deserves a frame...

There's no structure without boundaries, people can come and go without thought or difficulty. Having a path without boundaries when someone enters your life, provides the ability to take any form they like. Leaving no clear indication as to if they want you for you or you for the experience. You can't draw a conclusion until you draw the line, then you can feel when a person with childish ways is trying to color outside of those lines.

*Stop pledging allegiance to a **red flag**.*

Sometimes walking away from someone and walking in your purpose are the same thing. If you want your blessings in full, you must know how to part ways with part time people.

Whenever you take too long to cut a person off, God will make that very person stab you in the back so you get the point. Accepting a person for who they are doesn't always mean with open arms. Sometimes it means with distance, reflection, and realization.

*When the dots don't **connect**, **that's where** you draw the line.*

Stop giving ultimatums to people who haven't given you a thing.

Some people don't know what they have until what they have isn't having it anymore.

Budgeting isn't just about money, it's for your energy as well. Learn yourself and prioritize solely what contributes to your peace.

Some people don't know what they're missing because they never knew what they had. They couldn't see your true worth because you stretched it thin reaching for them.

When you worship the ground another person walks on and they walk all over you, take it as a sign to love yourself...

You rarely see people wash doormats, they just replace them when they're done. Doormats are used to clean the mess of a person's steps prior to crossing a threshold. They passively help people get to where they need to go, without regard. The next time you feel yourself being stepped on, cleanse yourself of that person.

If they're overly concerned with your past, leave them there.

Sometimes you have to burn a bridge to stay warm.

It's less about cutting people off, and more about removing yourself from a lifestyle that attracts those type of people. A lot of us are going elsewhere just to do the same things with the same type of people. A change of scenery doesn't always have to be about where you live, it's about how you spend your time and who you spend it with.

Be careful, the grass will always be greener over there when a person isn't showing you their true colors. Yes it's greener, but it isn't even grass, it's turf.

Learn the difference between a person being a work in progress and someone being a dead end job, being polished and being chipped away at. You cannot be a rock for a person who's just going with the flow. That stream will erode you over time and you'll be left up the creek wondering why you're in bad shape.

Stop allowing words to move you and actions to keep you in place, learn how to seek out motives. People will feed your insecurities just to fatten you up, so they can then feed off of you. Most don't actually want you, they just want validation. Only reaching out because they need you to pull them out of something. You can't entertain everyone who finds you attractive. A wolf is most genuine when approaching its prey, the most attractive at the moment, but the motive is deadly...

Just like a doctor's needle, people will inject themselves into your life to either give treatment or draw energy. Watch your symptoms and diagnose accordingly.

*Stop doing backflips **for people who have to flip** a coin for you.*

You treat yourself by the people you treat yourself to. Your circle isn't just about your friends, it's about your radius, your surroundings, what you keep around you, and what you entertain. Like a telescope, what you want to see in life depends on your circle. The circle of your eyepiece modifies your focus. If you want to change your circumstances, change your circumference.

The ones you need to keep around won't pull out an umbrella when you brainstorm, they'll help you channel those raindrops into the seeds you planted...

If you're waiting for a certain someone to realize your worth, you haven't realized it yet either.

When they don't believe that you're rare, make yourself scarce. Sometimes you have to show them the value of your presence in absence.

If everything that you miss of them is of the flesh, you aren't missing a thing.

Sometimes no matter how much you miss someone, you can't change the fact that they missed their chance. Like a drug addict goes through withdrawals, it's possible to miss someone who wasn't good for you, just don't relapse.

Stop seeking closure from people who couldn't be open with you.

Real loyalty glows in the dark.

If you have to investigate their loyalty, don't invest your time.

*When a person is giving you their all,
you don't have to piece things together.*

You have to be specific in what you ask for. A lot of us yearn for consistency in people, but truth be told, everyone is consistent. Some just consistently lie, backstab, and come up short.

Sometimes uncertainty is confirmation enough.

Your standards and worth are directly connected. To explain your worth is to dilute it. Whenever you have to take your worth down off the shelf to show someone, you're lowering your standards as well. Which will always be at eye level to a person who's on your level.

Your culture is your foundation. Culture is stripped to encourage blending with the masses. Unifying without knowing your culture is like getting into a relationship without knowing yourself, and we all know how that works out. It's dangerous because an entire body of people can be easily led to destruction under the disguise of salvation. When you know yourself, you know who's good for you and for what reason. Harmony is much more important than unity. We can all get along while thriving in our own settings. The only way people can truly contribute to humanity is by getting in touch with their culture. When we do that we will stand stronger in our strengths and be able to make change in solidarity.

In the midst of heartbreak, give your heart a break.

A broken heart is a vulnerable heart but it isn't an excuse to just let anything slip through the cracks. The wrong people will take advantage of that opening to take shelter and feed off of you. The right person will help you rebuild instead because they have enough foresight to know how beautiful you are when you're whole.

Amongst every broken heart lies peace of mind. You risk cutting yourself when you rush to pick up the pieces and fixate on why those things happened. This isn't how you fix it.

What if I told you the cracks in your heart are the routes of a map?

Sometimes we make heartbreak easier by neglecting the cracks that were already there. A broken heart, through an optimistic lens, is an opportunity to let your demons free. You can only do that when you take accountability and responsibility for your heart's current state...

That's how you turn a heartbreak into the hatching of new perspective.

There's a thin line between deceit and negligence. Ultimately, it's you who isn't giving you what you deserve.

Falling for potential has great potential for heartbreak.

Men live for today and women live for tomorrow. Some women are more prone to heartbreak and men tend to be the cause, sometimes unintentionally. In the sense of relationships, women are generally farsighted and fail to see red flags right in front of them. Distracted by emotions and potential too far out for the actual man to eclipse. And some men are too nearsighted to see the bigger picture of a future with a good woman through the convenience of what they don't have to focus on to witness per say.

*When you thought that they were your rock,
but they really were just a stepping stone.*

They were never solid. That's why they slipped through the cracks and evaporated on you when things got hot.

First they'll break you then act surprised when you cut them while they're trying to pick up the pieces...

*Why do we call disloyalty in a relationship "cheating?"
It should've never been a game to begin with...*

Sometimes your worth requires a growth that outweighs their ambition or just doesn't fit their path. And that's alright, that's why it may seem like a lot of your exes downgrade, because they run back to a comfort zone, rather than a space where they can evolve.

What you want wants something too.

Everybody wants to fish, but nobody wants to open up a can of worms.

Nothing worth it comes perfect. Your struggle is training you, not restraining you. You're either going to see your obstacles as punishment or as a training ground.

*What you're going through flows through you. Strengthening you so that you can hold on to what you want as long as you want. The steps you take on the path build your legs to push through the door. Things only become heavy when they come prematurely. When the world is on your shoulders, don't think of it as a burden, see it as an assignment that only you can carry. Somethings need to come with a process, as to access the ability to give **what you want what it needs**, so your breakthrough doesn't **eventually break you.**

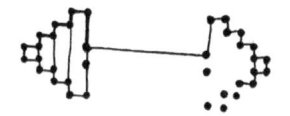

The world isn't telling you who you are, it's asking...

Dwelling on things you can't help isn't helping you.

Just because it didn't work out doesn't mean that it didn't work.

When you make a mistake, don't miss the chance to take the lesson. Stop counting your mistakes, and make them count.

You can't undo the past, but you can outdo it.

You'll go get it when you want it, not when you think you want it.

Pain is inevitable, it's consistent. Make sure that you are too. You know it's always going to visit, so meet it at the door and embrace it, but never let it in. It's temporary but you make it permanent when you hold on to it. The rain will come, but you prolong its effect when you fail to dry yourself off and keep it moving. Your tears can either drown you, or carry you ashore. What's done is done, but you aren't, and that's all that matters.

An open wound is an open door to an open mind.

When you minimize the perspective on a line graph, it will make a dip look like a drastic fall in the midst of a rise. Expand your perspective and keep your focus on the bigger picture.

The grass doesn't just change colors, the greener grass grows through the soil. Stop focusing so much on the surface level look of things, and give that greener grass time to grow through.

Sometimes the water for your seed will come as a storm.

Sometimes life has to bully you and turn your world upside down to shake the change out of you.

Life isn't about what you can take, it's about what you can give. People are stingy because they aren't big or strong enough to spare the loss. The greater you are, the more you can afford to give. That should be the motive you strive with.

Stop running from your demons. Their goal isn't always to catch you, it's to chase you off track. They're like bills, when you ignore them, they just grow with interest. You pay them off by paying them attention.

Potential is only potent when you know it.

Knowledge of a weakness is a strength depending on how you handle it. When you know your weaknesses, you can play into your strengths. Continuing to work on the lesser trait to avoid exposure through ignorance. In short, a weakness is just space for untapped potential. Learn yourself and go get it.

*Whenever darkness seems
to surround you, that's God
trying to get you to notice
your light within.*

Sometimes God will show you that you're on the right track through adversity.

That's a given because your true path is unbeaten...

You truly can't see what you're made of until you've been broken. Most of us have to learn how to make peace out of the pieces. The slab of rock doesn't just become a beautiful sculpture, it's chipped away at with persistence. Most importantly the sculpture is seen in the rock before the process even begins.

The difference between where you are now and where you want to be, is how you feel about it...

Discipline is important. It's your ability to not let your feelings dictate your movement.

The door that you need to get through isn't always locked, but your mind is. You don't possess the faith that it's already meant for you. Wipe your doubts at the door. And when you get through that door it doesn't mean there still isn't room for improvement. Keep pushing, the fruit of your labor isn't always to be eaten, it's to give you another seed to plant.

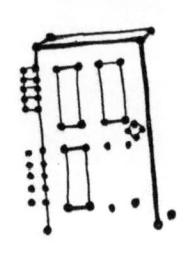

Everything that's on your mind will be found on your way. It can't be in your way until you're on your way, you can't truly have an obstacle without an objective. Your understanding of what comes together shapes what comes of your pursuit. You can't have something until it has you. Struggle is what truly pulls you out of you, not ease. So embrace everything that comes with it because it's everything that you asked for, even if you didn't envision it in its entirety. It's like the light at the end of the tunnel, the light is merely a symbol of your perspective at the time. It's small but it's also at its purest and as you progress, the light spreads, and you begin to see where you're going as the bigger picture is revealed. Then you realize, that the light was nothing in comparison. Finding yourself is so important, but the trick is that the path is what makes the introduction and ultimately builds your perspective to where your destiny receives everything it deserves out of you.

Love is a feeling. So to be in love is to be in your feelings. When you're in your feelings, you're vulnerable. When you're vulnerable, you're sensitive. When you're in a sensitive state, everything is magnified and exaggerated, good or bad.

Love is meant to reside within you, not the other way around.

There's not enough room for you, that's why being in love is also called being "caught up." This stretches the love prematurely instead of growing it, which leads to cracking and ultimately, to subconsciously premeditated heartbreak. Anguish which is self inflicted, but most will cast blame on the closest person to them; the person who they so irrationally jumped in love with rather than taking real account of their role in it...

Landing is an inevitable part of falling in love, and to think otherwise is ignorant. But why fall in love when you can stand for it?

The love you have for someone is easier to protect when you preside over it. When you do that, you can keep your logic with you, see that love in its entirety, witness all of its beauty, and also better diagnose issues with whom you share that love with. Instead of taking the risk of making your union a collateral casualty when that love eventually falls ill because you're too stuck inside of it.

Love is to be taken care of. And if you aren't right yourself, when you fall in love, you'll corrupt it with your very being. Again, love resides within you, when you take care of yourself, your love will benefit.

Just because you love someone doesn't mean you've found love. Where we go wrong is that we identify love with how we feel, and not how that other person feels and acts as well. We are too busy lost in our emotions because it feels awesome.

Only love can find love. Once your love meets its match, in motive and action, you've found love. But regardless, the most important love to find is the love we have for ourselves.

Whether you feel it now or later, you'll always strain yourself putting someone on a pedestal. Idolatry is the fast track to heartbreak. Worshiping the idea of someone rather than loving the real thing. Unfairly comparing that person to that idea, leading to the inevitable let down. Your love alone is enough when it comes to anything of the flesh. Love works in reality, while idolatry plays in fantasy. So love can see things for what they are, and nurture flaws accordingly, rather than trying to make a person bend to their will.

Stop trying to change the person you love, and change the way that you love them.

*If you choose it, love it.
If you love it, choose it.*

Loyal isn't a relationship status, it's a character trait.

It's less about being loyal to a person, and more about being faithful to a good moral code and placing your relationship within that...

The main person you need to take relationship advice from is the person you're with.

Nowadays, nobody wants to love the same way that they want to be loved. They want you to forgive them, but they want to be cut throat. They want you to understand, but never want to explain. They want you to accept them as they are, but need you to grow.

In a relationship, the only person who you should be afraid of losing is yourself.

Stop making alterations to your idea of love for unsuitable people. If they want to gain your affection, they'll lose the inches to fit into your future. People would rather conform completely to a person's interests before taking a risk and potentially putting them on to something new that they may love by being themselves.

In football, when you're running a pass route and the throw is off, you have to come off of your path to make the catch. The best passes meet you where you're headed. This can also be applied to your relationships with people. If you have be someone who you're not to gain acceptance, **that is** *getting you off of your path like* **that** *bad throw. But unlike football,* **you** *shouldn't want to go for that* **bad pass.**

Love is unconditional, but that doesn't mean that the relationship should be.

Communication doesn't make the relationship, it takes it where it needs to go.

Trust the commute...

The best teachers are continuous students. You have to learn in order to teach, learn as in get to know your student. So you can reach them where they are, and guide them on their personal path to the desired destination. It's like a group of people planning to meet somewhere but coming from different places. Your GPS will give you a route dependent on your current location. You have to know the landscape or big picture in its entirety if you want to reach people. This is how communication should work. When you're in a relationship, understanding your partner is like getting their coordinates, you know where they're coming from when they say certain things to you. And you know how to present things to them so it translates through their perception in a way that truly builds understanding.

A big part of putting someone first is simply giving them a second thought.

Know the difference between someone who always has to be right and someone who wants to be right for you. If they have to be right all the time, they can't possibly want to be right for you.

Ironically, what a person sees in you is more important than how they look.

Stop allowing people to talk their way into your heart. Your love isn't password accessible, make them pick the lock.

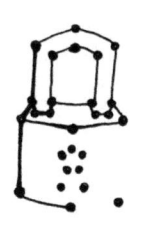

Equity isn't just for property, it can be applied to relationships as well. The more a person invests in it, the more trust will accrue. There's a thin line between instinct and business. At the foundation of every relationship we encounter, there's some form of trade. The only difference is the quality and quantity of the assets offered from both parties, including the emotions they bring. Some of us simply just make bad investment decisions. Once you realize this, you'll stop taking everything so personal. The more you recognize the similarities, the less you'll find yourself in compromising positions.

Women respect power, so when a man shows that he doesn't have power over temptation, it's a turn off.

Submission is less a gender thing, and more a strengths and weaknesses thing. Where you excel, I concede and learn. Where I excel, you concede and learn. And we become stronger together.

If you can't submit, don't commit.

Submission isn't weakness, distorted judgment of character is. Focus more on the flawed thought process that simply picks the wrong person rather than the acts that follow.

Part of the reason why our relationships aren't working, is because there isn't a clear consistent code gender wide on both sides. This creates a wide range of options because if a man or woman has issues, they won't stay and face them. They'd rather call it quits because they know they can find someone who'll put up with it.

To love is to have love. Love is its own cause and effect, a noun and more importantly a verb, which is often overlooked. A lot of us solely depend on the feeling to get us through, but that will never last. Because the feeling of love feeds off the action of love. The friendship, the loyalty, the communication, the forgiveness, the faith, and most importantly the effort all embody the action of love which serves as the catalyst to actually feel love. Love, the feeling, should inspire the action and vice versa. Love is both the root and the fruit. Without the desire to explore a person and truly get to their core, how can you validate the feeling of true love?

Love yourself then find someone who understands why...

*Love is a dance and sometimes **you'll step on each other's toes**. But as long as **you keep your hands around each other**, you'll **make it to a better song**.*

Your words will always sentence you accountable when your actions don't spell it out. To claim that you're a product of your environment, as an excuse to your detriment, is to admit defeat. If you were a product of your environment, you would learn it, adapt, and maneuver accordingly to circumvent it, succeed, and come back to make your environment a product of you.

Entitlement is a delusion that will often lead you to overly focus on the way you think things should be, rather than the way things actually are. There's nothing wrong with having aspirations but you cannot live in them, you have to live in reality, and work to make it what you want it to be. Some people believe that they should be accepted for who they are so much that it stunts their growth. We think everything is supposed to be given when this world doesn't owe us a thing. The very breath you breathe is the biggest blessing you'll ever receive. So when you think about it, we all come out with more than we deserve. While you cry yourself a river, your time continues to float up the creek. A lot of us compare ourselves right into insecurity, jealousy, and bitterness. Because our perspective is skewed, we aren't raised to praise the right things. Our parents aren't in full attendance because they're too caught up in the hamster wheel of a commercial society. They mean well but it isn't enough. Consequently, causing children to fall into materialism instead of learning themselves through loving arms. This failure leads to love being misplaced somewhere it'll never fit, which brings eternal internal yearning that'll forever be disappointed. Deep rooted issues keep us stagnant because staying in shallow waters keep us from facing them. A shallow mind is easily manipulated by outside forces as they don't have to go as far. These forces steer us to excuses so much that we excuse ourselves right from the table that feeds us.

Cutting corners won't give you the edge.

Don't mistaken responsibility for your actions with responsibility for the consequences. Responsibility for your actions is self aware. Your ability to choose right from wrong is solely under your control, and not dictated by your situation. A lot of us are acting out of dependent personality and not out of independent character. You have the choice to choose. Making mistakes is alright, but make them out of a lack of knowledge, not a lack of good judgment. Stop minimizing your life down to your current situation or surroundings.

You're not a product, you're the source.

*When you manifest and nurture your energy, you don't just create something that those around you can feel, but something that can feel back. In other words, energy that's intimately cultivated gives you a reliable baseline to differentiate any and everything that enters your zone. It'll tell you who and what moves in harmony or acts to harm. When you have demons of your own, it's easier for someone else's to just blend in with the crowd. A healthy structured environment is the solution to a lot of our issues nowadays. It gives the troubled something to lean on because when anything goes, there are no barriers. So there's also no guard against the evils that dwell. But you can't rightfully do that until you get a palette based in reality and logic, which comes with embracing the truth. The truth is like smelling coffee beans to reset the sense of smell when trying to figure out which scents that you agree with or not. A lot of us make bad decisions because **we don't have an actual decision making process, we just let our emotions run the show.***

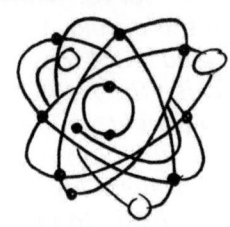

*A lot of our thoughts **begin from the back door of imagi**nation rather than the front **door of reason and that's why we find** ourselves misled in so many situations. Mistakes don't start where the eyes can see, they're conceived in your thought process. So if you want to be better, just think. Decision making should be a process, not just a feeling. How you feel should be a part of your decision making process but not the only component. Morals, logic, and foresight should act as the front line with our feelings behind them. Giving us time to settle as all feelings are exaggerated in the beginning of any event. And allowing that front line to breakdown an event to the point where our emotions can feel a situation for what it purely is. When you catch feelings, hold them awhile and give some thought to how you use them. Time names emotion, some names are just longer or harder to write out than others. When you give things time, things give you understanding in return, which is the only justifiable exchange for time spent. Feelings are fleeting, just like most things in life. Being in your feelings isn't an excuse to get out of character. Recognize the set up in getting upset. A lot of us prolong the bad because we allow our feelings to consume us like they're here to stay. Just be patient, give things time, and let them pass in peace.*

You can't become whole without your peace.

*There's no power without peace.
There's no peace without accountability.*

They didn't make you mad, sad, or happy. You chose those feelings. Instead of transferring energy into an empty void through blame, close the circuit by pointing at yourself.

That's literal empowerment.

"i" will always find myself detached unless "I" learn how to stand alone.

Your morals, principles, and values are called "what you stand on" for a reason. Where and how you stand dictates your perspective, which defines important elements like loyalty, love, and success. No matter the effort, if you don't stand on the same things, you'll never see eye to eye. Sometimes principle and emotion don't meet in agreement. But in that same breath, feelings can drive principle. When you truly love something or someone, your logic strengthens your consideration and regard. When you're dictated by emotions, in most cases, you'll run the red light of those intersections.
Keeping logic at the forefront is like a driving instructor letting you drive but having a brake pedal on their side just in case.

A small mind is easy to lose.

The more you understand the less you overreact.

What you entertain enters you, be careful.

You can't break the cycle because you're too concerned with staying in the loop.

Once you stop forcing it, you become a force to be reckoned with. To try to fit in with anything unnaturally is to limit your form. Whenever you're trying to keep up with something like trends, gossip, accomplishments of others, love interests, etc., you subconsciously put yourself in a second place position. But when you focus on being yourself, you put yourself first. What goes around comes around. So stand still, still as in true to yourself. If not, you're doomed to chase something you'll never catch, instead of being ahead of the curve by standing in your purpose. You'll never be satisfied looking for the next best thing. But you'll always be fulfilled when you focus on what you have, what's meant for you, and building a life where those things can thrive. Self validation is important because without it you'll be easily swayed by insults as well as compliments and never able to move on your own accord. Knowing your worth doesn't just shield you from hate, it puts love in its proper perspective to the point where it doesn't confirm **ego and can truly be appreciated.**

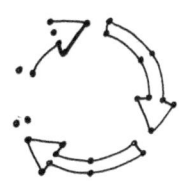

You can't stand in your peace when you're still lying to yourself.

Getting to know yourself is important when you're itching for more out of life. But you get what you give. And when you only scratch the surface of your mind and soul, you limit what you can give the world and a significant other. It's hard to take anyone's breath away sitting in shallow waters.

Go explore your ocean.

Once you begin to follow the path traced for you, what's meant for you will be drawn to you.

You only have to put on a hard exterior when your inner self is out of order, vulnerable, and weak. When your soul is centered inside an acute spirit, there's no need for fear or any other protection. For the truth can never be threatened.

Throwing shade won't take away from the darkness that you're in...

No matter how well the weight is distributed, a scale won't achieve balance if the equilibrium is off. Peace isn't about everything being good, it's about seeing the good in everything. Peace is right outside of your feelings, just get out of them. Happiness is a product of peace, not the other way around. The pursuit of happiness is a dead end road. It's a fleeting feeling that you'll be chasing forever, constantly trying to duplicate that high. Happiness isn't yours to possess, it's yours to witness and enjoy. It's attracted to contentment for it knows it'll truly be appreciated. Build a state of peace instead. It'll keep you grounded as those feelings come and go.

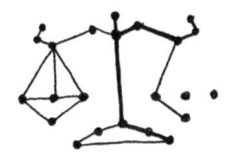

*Stop trying to dodge **raindrops** **when** you're dying of thirst.*

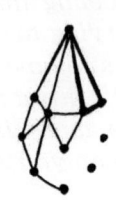

We tend to identify victims solely as people who've lost something. But the biggest victims are the ones who can't let go of anything.

People aren't made to hold energy, we're made to channel it. This is why people project insecurities, fear, and anger. Be intentional with your circle, surroundings, and time. To take accountability and relinquish glory is energy transference. The ego will always try to hoard and overcompensate because it thrives in the limits of the flesh. When your faith stands in something higher than yourself, your spirit will preside in abundance and find peace in the fact that there's always more where that came from, especially when you know how to channel it properly. Emotions are energy in motion. We can't always control what calls for our energy. But we can choose the direction that we send it in, which is the only thing that separates the various types of emotion. A sucker for love is just a person that's dictated by their emotions to fall irrationally. But the thing about being emotionally dictated, is that it also applies when that emotion turns into anger, sadness, lust, etc. causing you to do some things you can't take back. Keep your logic first and don't let your emotions have you.

*The funny thing about not paying attention is that **it'll still cost** you.*

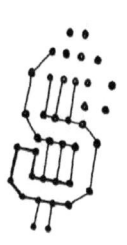

Just because you can't see the sun doesn't mean it isn't out. Something is just blocking your view, but you can still feel its heat. A lot of us feel something within ourselves but the ego won't believe it until it presents itself. What is within you is just as absolute as the sun. It has always been there, just focus on clearing your skies.

Your hands will always try to see what your eyes can't reach. Be careful, your eyes aren't your guide, they are only a window to see where your heart should be taking you. Try to take the time to listen to what you see and look at what you hear. In other words, always question why you see things the way that you do, and always read what you hear back to you at least once over.

The black cat isn't bad luck. Your belief in it being bad luck just alters your focus, so you relay all the inevitable bad back to that black cat. It's almost like when you're in the market for a certain model of car, then you start seeing that particular model everywhere. The cars don't just pop out of the ground, your focus is just different. With that being said, use that knowledge to your advantage, take control of your thinking, and focus more on the positive.

Once you begin to see issues from a three dimensional perspective instead of a two dimensional face value, you'll be able to digest complexities and realize the multiple rights and wrongs that can exist within an argument. Thus, learning when you're actually facing an ally with a different perspective, rather than an opposition where you can take advantage of this understanding and learn from one another. Real intelligence presides in nuance, not extremes.

Nuance is a vital root of understanding. It's the gray area in a society that teaches you that the world is black and white and demands you pick a side. There's no balance in that, therefore it doesn't get you anywhere but a dead end. That's why programming is so dangerous, it manipulates emotion to carry you to various extremes. Truly knowing right from wrong is vital to being able to pick out the good from two opposing sides, filter out the bad, and find a middle ground.

Sugar coating will only lead to more cavities.

Positive vibes only is cool, but unbalanced and unnatural in reality. You have to stay aware of the negatives to circumvent them. Being self aware is less about praising your strengths and more about recognizing, embracing, and working on your flaws.

Learn the difference between fact and opinion. When you're checking yourself, you have to diagnose your condition under the light of truth. A lot of us accept or reject truth based on how we feel about it, but your feelings don't change the truth. That can't continue, there's no growth there. The sun doesn't just provide a sprouting seed with nutrients, it serves as a guiding light showing which direction to grow towards. The truth always comes to light. You're still in the dark because you're living a lie.

Honesty will always bring division because the truth inevitably forms a partition in the variety of opinion. In the end, that division undresses an honest unity because you know who's who. There's a certain honest order to chaos and destruction, as they both contribute to destiny.

Whenever you make a mistake, selfishness will want to go back before anyone found out, maturity will want to go back before you committed the act, but peace won't want to go back at all.

Good or bad, intentions will outweigh actions. A person with deceptive intent will act accordingly. A person with the best intentions is going to make mistakes; sometimes the very definition of a mistake changes with intention. Once you become whole, you'll push truth up against the surface of your being, making honesty easier. The more broken apart you are, the more prone you are to reach for anything and even make things up to cling to, making deceit effortless.

The fight between your lower and higher self will always come down to a decision...

Your conscience is segmented between your lower and higher self. The key to accessing your potential is simple, obey the voice of your higher self. Understanding the difference between the two voices is key. The higher self is usually challenging, it's that voice that tells you to do the right thing, even when it'll bear no fruit; like picking up the trash that isn't yours. The lower self is the comfort zone, where demons thrive in refuge. They can be heard, but not seen, as they work to distract you from hearing your higher self. The more you listen to your higher self, the more light you will shed minimizing the lower self and ridding yourself of those demons. Get away from the noise, find that voice, and follow it.

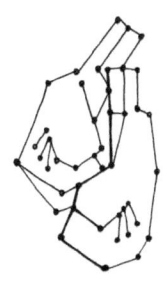

You don't change the puzzle piece, you change its placement. You're the missing piece somewhere, go find your place...

Happiness is a gift that you give yourself when you live in the present.

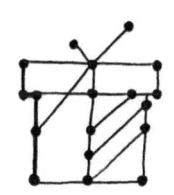

*Success doesn't always bring happiness,
but happiness is always a success.*

You aren't seeing any harvest because you're holding on to your seeds.

If you want to succeed in life, you have to take risks. Even the caterpillar has to go out **on a limb to form a cocoon.**

Discipline is most tested when the positive results start rolling in.

Be mindful, too much celebration can turn your momentum in the wrong direction...

You'll never find the needle in the haystack when you're scared of being poked by it...

In basketball, all good defenders run the risk of being crossed. The guy who plays it safe will keep his ankles but he will never make an NBA All Defensive team.

Whenever you take risks, you risk failure, but you also expose yourself to success.

There's a difference between proactive wisdom and reactive wisdom. Reactive wisdom teaches you how to avoid the potholes, but proactive wisdom teaches you how to fix the road. Reactive wisdom may keep you above water, but proactive wisdom shows you how to build a boat. Both are vital, but more so solution-oriented proactive wisdom to pass down to our children and push generations forward.

There's always a risk in wanting something you've never had. But that's why knowing yourself is important. A lot of people want the mountaintop, but will discover that they're scared of heights. You have to learn how to plan ahead of achievement. Nowadays, most people's motivations for what they do in life come from jealousy and boredom. And that isn't grounds for true success or fulfillment. Success requires a process. Every process requires routine, the building blocks of consistency. Although sometimes routines get boring, they're vital in the long run. When you let the feelings of jealousy and boredom dictate your movements, they'll take you on an assortment of short sprints in arbitrary directions, ultimately wasting energy and time. There will always be someone that seems further along, something within reach that seems better, or times that aren't the most fun. But when your motives are rooted in purpose, you're only focused on what's for you. For example, a lot of people flop and sink into debt and drugs after "success" because the goal took sole precedence and when they got it, there was nothing else to look forward to. More importantly, they tied their entire worth to a destination, instead of purpose, just to realize that place wasn't what they thought indirectly making **their worth** *questionable.*

There's a thin line between ambition and greed.

What's the rush with something that you want forever?

Whether it's with goals, significant others, etc., people rush things because they don't intend on staying long. They're trying to get what they can before they're exposed. If you want certain things for a lifetime and not just a moment, you have to see the lifetime in a moment. When you aim to create revenue and teach others to reach their dreams by doing the same, your evaluation can never be measured, it's endless. Instead of chasing something pursue understanding and use that understanding to be what that something needs. Pursue and study it. Become the attraction of your desires, and work to present your authentic self.

Running after a rabbit isn't going to be effective. Go get you a carrot, lay a trap, and be patient.

To be consistent is to make sure what you bring to the table never changes for the worse, no matter how those tables turn. It may change the way that certain something looks, but the effort stays the same.

Acting out will always get you some attention. But not acting at all, will get you the right attention. This society leads us to focus on the external but neglect the internal, which is the attention we give ourselves from the inside out. Reflection will keep you grounded in a world that tells you to jump through hoops for validation. When you care too much about what people think, you start to think like them. Then those thoughts become things that aren't really meant for you. Leaving you to wonder why nothing seems right, it's because you aren't thinking for yourself.

Beauty begins with "bea u" for a reason.

Time isn't money, it's worth more. Making money is great and important in this society, of course. But if you understand business and how profit margins work, you know that you'll never get your money's worth with anything ever. Your time is priceless until you exchange it for something, then you establish its value in that instance. Like an hourglass, you have to take things with a grain of salt when your time is your value.

Don't wait for life to come to you, come to life.

Sometimes, your best foot forward is the one that you place in another person's shoes.

To do right only when someone is watching is wrong. To do right only so that you can look at yourself in the mirror will not inspire a worthy reflection. To do right only because you think enough right turns will bring something positive full circle isn't how karma works. Karma couldn't care less about your actions, it's your motives that motivate what you deserve.

Every now and then, all that you seek will be under the new leaf that you need to turn over.

In order to move forward in life, you must know how to identify a stage, discover its purpose, and lastly, say goodbye at the appropriate time.

Sometimes the little things are big enough.

Stop obsessing about the light at the end of the tunnel, access your light from within, and enjoy the writing on the wall.

Life is too short for a short temper. So much so, it's easy to overlook sometimes. That's why we get on our knees to give thanks. The blessing is less about what you have, and more about what you don't have to put up with. Sometimes a brush with death is needed to paint the picture of life, the way it should be. To know that your days are numbered is how you make them count. Once you realize how fragile life is, you'll reach a breakthrough. If you're alive, you're winning. Everything around you is a bonus, so treat them as such, and be thankful for every moment above ground. As long as you have breath in your lungs, you'll always have a blessing to count. And as long as your heart beats, you can beat anything. Learn to appreciate life. No matter what kind of hand that you're dealt, always send your thank you card.

We are all on borrowed time. And just like with money, it's usually for a reason. You're here for a reason, find it and pay it forward...

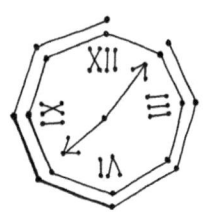

Thank you.